BREEDERS

Ben Hoare

Raintree
Chicago, Illinois

First published 2003 by Raintree, a division of Reed Elsevier Inc.
© 2003 The Brown Reference Group plc

Library of Congress Cataloging-in-Publication Data

Hoare, Ben.
  Breeders / Ben Hoare.
    p. cm. — (Parasites and partners)
Summary: A comprehensive look at different types of creatures that use
other creatures or plants as part of their reproduction, such as flowers
that require insects for pollination, or birds that lay eggs in other birds nests.
Includes bibliographical references and index.
  ISBN 0-7398-6986-8 (lib. bdg.-hardcover) – ISBN 1-4109-0353-2 (pbk.)
  1. Mutualism (Biology)—Juvenile literature. [1. Symbiosis. 2.
Animals—Habits and behavior.] I. Title. II. Series.
  QH548.3.H63 2003
  577.8'52—dc21

                    2003007050

ISBN 0-7398-6986-8

Printed and bound in Singapore.
1 2 3 4 5 6 7 8 9 0 07 06 05 04 03 02

Acknowledgements

The publisher would like to thank the following for permission to use photographs:

Key: l – left, r – right, c – center, t – top, b – bottom.
Africa Media Online: Nigel Dennis/Africa Imagery 9b; **Bat Conservation International:** Merlin D. Tuttle 10b; **Bruce Coleman Collection:** Joe McDonald 26, Kim Taylor 7; **Corbis:** Ron Boardman/FLPA 8t, Michael & Patricia Fogden 12b, Paul Funston/Gallo Images 5c, Francesco Muntada 24b; **Sean Evans:** 28t; **Lalangi Jayawardhana:** 14b; **Image Ideas:** 5b; **Jeff Jeffords:** 4bc; **Natural Science Photos:** J. Burgess 8b, C. Dani & I. Jeske 18b, C. & T. Stuart 13t, John W. Warden 25b; **Nature Picture Library:** Jim Clare 9t, Jeff Foott 25t; **NHPA:** N. A. Callow 29, Bill Coster 28b, E. A. Janes 24t, Ralph & Daphne Keller 20b, Christophe Ratier 13b, Norbert Wu 20t; **Oxford Scientific Films:** Robin Bush 11t, Mark Deeble & Victoria Stone 23, Peter Gathercole 18t, Karen Gowlett-Holmes 19, Tim Jackson 14-15, Stan Osolinski 17; **PHIL:** CDC/Janice Carr 4b; **Photodisc:** Photolink 12t, 14t; **Still Pictures:** 10t; **USDA/ARS:** Scott Bauer, 4ct, Jack Dykinga 4t, Eric Erbe & Chris Pooley 30; **USFWS:** Dave Menke 5t
Front Cover: Nature Picture Library: Jeff Foott (t); **Oxford Scientific Films:** Robin Bush (b)

For The Brown Reference Group

Project Editor: Jim Martin
Consultancy Board: Dr. Kimberley N. Russell, Division of
    Invertebrate Zoology, American Museum of Natural
    History, New York; Prof. Marilyn Scott, Institute of
    Parasitology, McGill University, Montreal, Canada
Designed by: Pewter Design Associates
Illustrator: Mike Woods
Picture Researcher: Helen Simm
Managing Editor: Bridget Giles
Art Director: Dave Goodman
Production Director: Alastair Gourlay

Raintree

Editor: Jim Schneider
Managing Editor: Jamie West
Production Manager: Brian Suderski

Front cover: A yellow warbler struggles to feed both a large
cowbird chick and her own brood (*top*); a Northland green
gecko feeds on flower nectar (*bottom*).

Title page: A stick insect nymph scurries free from the ants'
nest in which it hatched from its egg.

Note to the Reader
Some words are shown in bold, like **this.** You can find out what they mean by looking in "Words to Know."

Contents

Introduction

Animals and plants do not live alone. They are always interacting with other creatures. A close association between different species is called a **symbiosis.** *Parasites & Partners* introduces you to symbiotic relationships. You can see examples of these around you every day. Anyone who keeps a dog shares a symbiosis with their pet. The dog is fed and housed by its owner, who gains a companion and protection in return. Both partners in this relationship benefit, but that is not always the case. The different types of symbioses covered in this book are discussed in the box below.

Each book in *Parasites & Partners* looks at a different group of relationships. Find out how plants and animals interact with other types of creatures as they feed, breed, keep clean, find a home, and move around.

Some important words for you to remember

Symbiosis

A relationship between two different types of creatures is called a symbiosis. This bee is taking nectar from the flower to feed its young, while the plant is using the bee to spread its pollen. Both partners benefit in this example.

Mutualism

Biologists call a relationship in which both partners benefit a **mutualism.** Leaf-cutter ants provide food in the form of chewed-up leaves, and a safe home for their fungus partners. The ants get to eat parts of the fungi in return.

Commensalism

A relationship in which one **organism** benefits but the other neither profits nor suffers is called a **commensalism.** One of the partners is usually called a host. Here, a crinoid shrimp blends in with the colors of its feather star host.

Parasite

A creature that benefits at the expense of another but does not usually kill it is called a **parasite.** The organisms they attack are called hosts. This flea is a rat parasite. It lives on the body of a rat and feeds on its blood.

4

◀ *This is a female wood duck. She may lay a clutch of eggs sneakily in the nest of another wood duck. Discover nature's cheats and tricksters on **pages 22–29**.*

▼ *A fresh pile of elephant dung is soon covered with dung beetles. The dung forms a beetle nursery. Learn about animals that breed with the help of others on **pages 16–21**.*

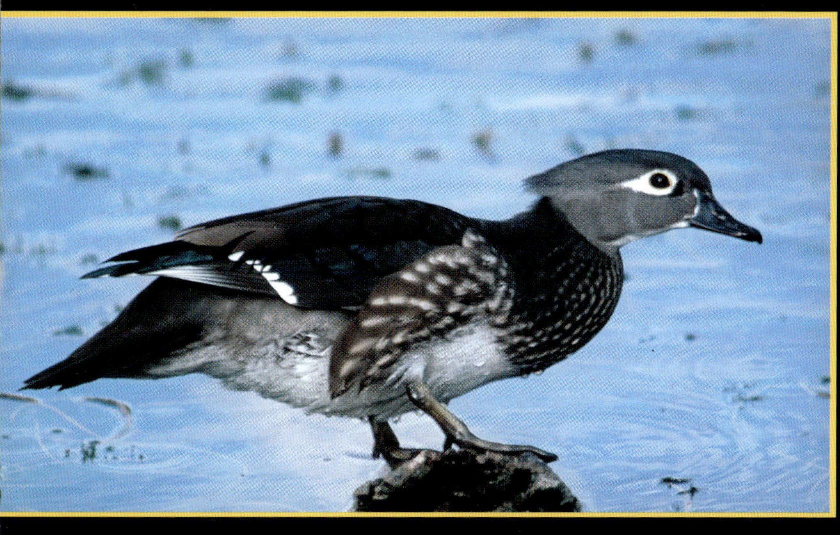

In **this** book...

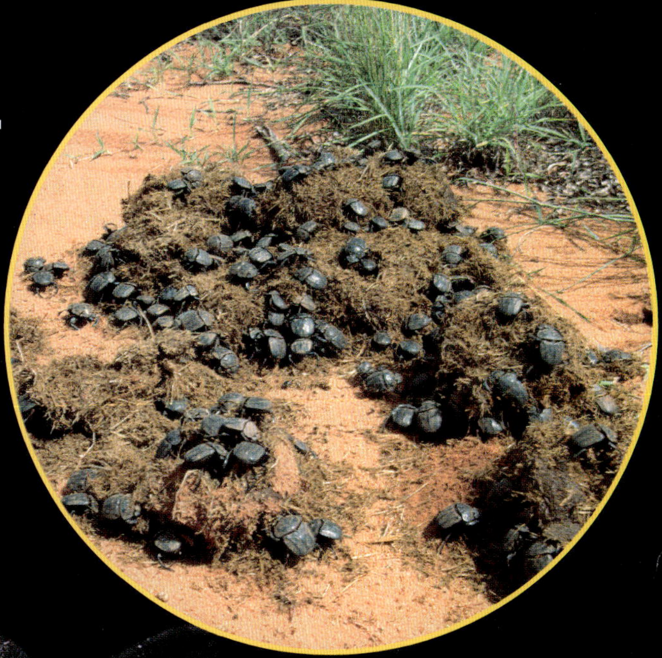

...you will look at animals and plants that need other creatures to help them breed. The relationship may be equal, with both partners benefiting, but sometimes one partner exploits the other. In chapter one, we learn about the ways plants use animals to spread their pollen and seeds, often offering a reward in return.

Chapter two looks at animals that need other animals to help them breed. Some animals provide dung that forms beetle nurseries. Others share nests, and some develop inside other animals.

In the final chapter, we discover how plants and animals such as cuckoos, stick insects, and mirror orchids trick other creatures to help them breed.

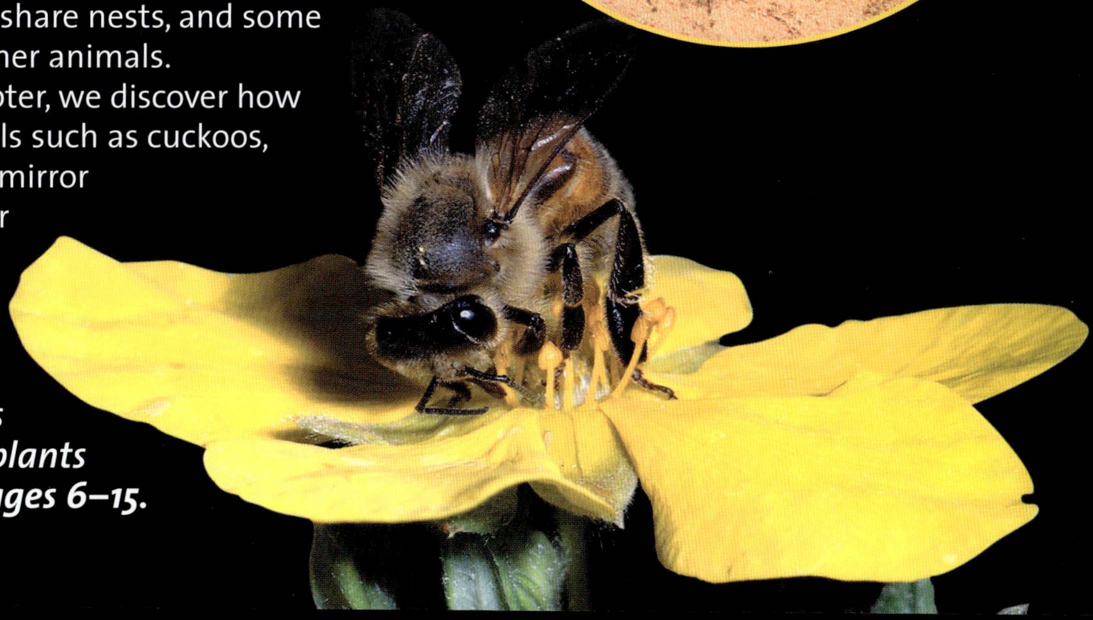

▶ *Find out how animals like this honeybee help plants reproduce on **pages 6–15**.*

Flower **POWER**

Plants form partnerships with all kinds of creatures, such as bees, monkeys, bats, birds, and even fish. These animals help the plants reproduce but often demand a meal in return. Millions of different species depend on partnerships like these to survive.

The flowers of plants are not just for show—they play a vital role in the **reproduction** of these plants. Flowers usually have both male and female parts. The male part makes **pollen.** This is a fine powder that contains male sex cells. If pollen from one flower enters the female part of another, it can **fertilize** (fuse with) the female sex cells.

The transfer of pollen between flowers is called **pollination.** Without this transfer, flowering plants cannot produce seeds. Plants transfer their pollen in many ways.

Some plants, such as grasses, rely on gusts of wind. Others use animals called **pollinators** to carry pollen for them. But pollinators do not do the job for free, so plants offer food as payment. This is a fair deal, since the animals know that if they visit a flower, a meal will be waiting. Most pollination relationships are **mutualisms,** since both partners benefit.

Incredible insects

Most pollinators are insects. Insects make ideal pollen carriers. There are vast numbers of insects, and many can fly between flowers.

▼ *A hoverfly feeds on a kingcup flower's nectar. Pollen attaches to hairs on the fly's body.*

▲ Ragwort pollen seen under a microscope. The pollen fertilizes the sex cells of a female flower, enabling seeds to be produced.

Insects also live almost everywhere. There are insects that pollinate flowers in the freezing Arctic, at the tops of high mountains, and in scorching hot deserts.

Busy as a bee

Honeybees are well-known pollinators. These insects live in nests called hives. Each hive contains a queen bee, about 50,000 female workers, several hundred males, and lots of **larvae** (young). Young workers look after the nest, but older ones do more dangerous work. They venture out to collect pollen and **nectar** (a sweet liquid) from flowers for their nest mates to eat.

Bulging baskets

A worker bee's body is covered with microscopic hooks. The hooks pick up pollen grains as the bee crawls over flowers. The bee often stops to comb the pollen into parts of its back legs called pollen baskets. When its pollen baskets are full, the bee returns to the hive.

Swarms of worker bees buzz back and forth between the hive and nearby flowers. Although the bees carry away a lot of the pollen, a little rubs off whenever they land on a flower. Just a few tiny grains of pollen are enough to pollinate the flowers visited by the bees.

Thirsty work

To tempt visitors, many flowers offer nectar as well as pollen. Nectar is a thick, sweet syrup that oozes into a funnel-shaped part of the flower. Many animals find it irresistible. Butterflies and moths suck it up through a long tube called the **proboscis.** This works like a drinking straw. The proboscis coils neatly under the head when not in use.

◄ The yellow lump on this worker honeybee is a ball of pollen that has been packed into a pollen basket.

▶ A sword-billed humming-bird uses its extremely long tongue to reach sugary nectar deep inside a flower.

Hyperactive hummers

Many birds love nectar, including the hummingbirds of North and South America. Hummingbirds hover in front of flowers and sip the nectar with their long tongues. As the birds feed, feathers on their heads become covered with sticky pollen.

Hummingbirds are always on the move, darting from flower to flower in a blur. They may beat their wings up to 90 times each second! Flying like this requires a huge amount of energy, so a hummingbird must drink more than half its body weight in nectar each day.

Hungry animals cannot afford to go to the wrong type of flower. A hummingbird would find it impossible to feed from a daisy, for example, since its bill would not fit the flower. Plants must also attract the right pollinators. They often do this by advertising with bright colors and powerful perfumes. Some plants attract a variety of pollinators, while others attract only a few types, or even just one.

Tempting smells

Insects have a good sense of smell and use it to tell flowers apart. Flowers may smell soft and delicate, or rich and fruity. A few reek of dung or urine. The dead horse arum plant smells like rotting flesh. It tricks flies that like to lay their eggs inside dead animals into paying a visit. The flies then pollinate the flower. This is a **parasitic** relationship. The plant benefits, but the flies waste time and energy visiting the plant.

Insects also have superb vision. They can detect **ultraviolet** colors that are invisible to people. Many flowers have ultraviolet dots and lines on their petals that guide insects to the nectar inside.

▼ Protea plant nectar is a vital food source for a Cape sugarbird. The bird pollinates the flowers as it feeds.

9

The big stink

The world's largest flower belongs to *Rafflesia*, a parasitic plant found in Southeast Asia. For years at a time, this monster lurks inside the tissues of plants that hang down from rain forest trees. Eventually, *Rafflesia* bursts out and opens a massive red flower. The flower measures up to 3 feet (0.9 m) across and weighs about 20 pounds (9 kg). The flower gives off a revolting stench like rotting fish. This attracts clouds of black flies. As the flies swarm into the bloom's smelly central chamber, pollen grains stick to their backs. When the flies visit a different *Rafflesia*, they transfer the pollen and fertilize the flower. The flies are tiny, so it is a mystery why the flowers are so big!

▶ *The world's largest flower,* Rafflesia, *draws in pollinating flies with a powerful stench.*

Birds have a poor sense of smell. Plants that need to attract them usually do not waste energy on perfume production. But birds have excellent eyesight. They look out for boldly colored flowers and are particularly tempted by red and orange blooms.

The night shift

In warm parts of the world, many plants use bats as pollinators. The flowers of these plants open after sunset. Without the need for colors to attract their nighttime

▶ *This lesser long-nosed bat will use its long tongue to feed on cactus nectar.*

visitors, these flowers are usually white, but they can have very powerful smells. Wild banana trees are pollinated by fruit bats. The flowers of these trees dangle down on long stalks, allowing the bats easy access.

A host of other animals feast on nectar at night. The Northland green gecko from New Zealand, for example, clambers up manuka plants to lick nectar from their flowers. Its head soon becomes smeared with pollen.

Fussy flowers

Some flowers are choosy about whom they invite for dinner. They have such an unusual shape that only one species of animal can feed from them.

Madagascar star orchids grow tubes up to 11 inches (28 cm) deep. Nectar collects at the bottom of the tubes. Nothing can reach this nectar except a type of hawk moth. The moth's proboscis extends up to four times the length of its body. The flower cannot reproduce without the hawk moth, while the moth cannot feed on any other plant.

Flowers such as the pink gentian have particularly fine pollen. When a visiting carpenter bee lands on the flower, it vibrates its wings at a very precise speed. This dislodges the pollen from the flower. Only the carpenter bee can gain access to the flower's pollen.

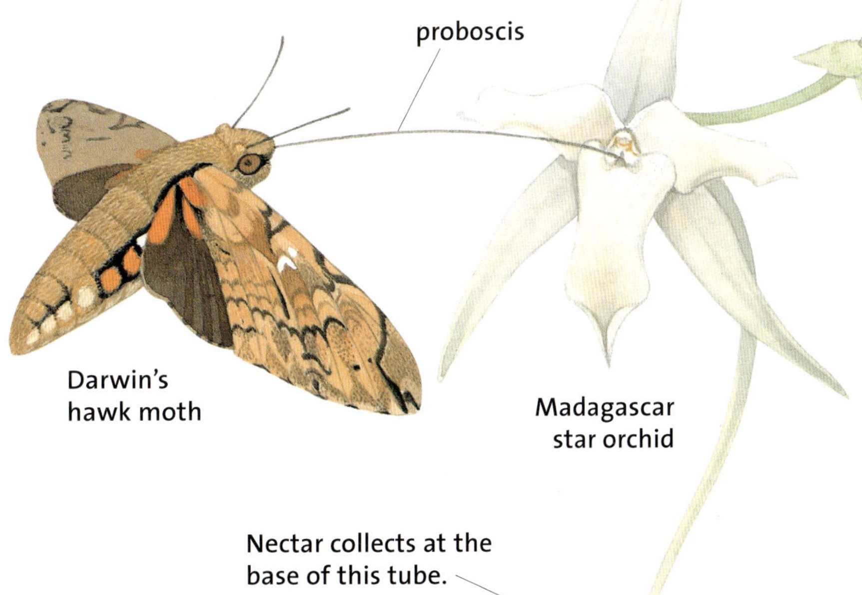

▲ *A water lily flower can become a prison for pollinating beetles.*

▼ *A female yucca moth inside a yucca flower.*

Perfect partners

Yucca plants share a particularly close relationship with yucca moths. The female moth lays her eggs inside yucca flowers. The caterpillars only feed on yucca seeds. To ensure a supply of seeds for her young, the yucca moth stuffs a little ball of pollen into the female parts of a yucca flower. Without this deliberate pollination, the yucca could not produce seeds, and the caterpillars would starve.

Beetle kidnappers

Some plants kidnap insects to make sure they do the job. Fragrant water lily flowers open before their pollen is ready. Visiting beetles tumble into a pool of liquid inside the flower. The fluid draws away any pollen that is attached to the bodies of the beetles and channels it to the female parts of the flower. Once pollinated, the flower stops producing fluid and releases its own pollen. The lilies then allow their insect captives to escape.

Sowing the seed

Pollination is not the only reason that plants form partnerships with animals. They use animals to scatter their seeds, too. Again, animals will not transport the cargo for free. Many plants surround their seeds with juicy fruit as a reward.

When an animal eats the soft flesh of a fruit, it usually swallows some of the tough seeds as well. These travel into the animal's stomach and pass out later in its droppings. By that time, the animal has moved to a different place. This is important for the seeds. If they grew in the shade of their parent's leaves they would be starved of light and die. Movement of **organisms** to new areas is called **dispersal.**

Fruits of the forest

Sugary fruit is an important and delicious forest food. When chimpanzees discover a tree laden with ripe fruit they hoot and scream with excitement. Squabbles break out over the best feeding spots.

The chimps are messy eaters and drop lots of the fruit, but it does not go to waste. Small antelopes called duikers follow

▲ Fallen fruit is dispersed by animals of the forest floor, such as this Ader's duiker.

parties of foraging chimps through the forest. The duikers feast on the fallen fruit. Both the chimps and the duikers help disperse the seeds.

Sweet sensation

Piranha fish are well known as fierce **predators** of fish and other animals in the waters of the Amazon River. But most types of piranhas are gentle fish that rely on fallen fruit for food.

For several months each year, the Amazon rises over its banks and the forest is flooded. The fish swim over the forest floor. They listen for the plop of fruit falling into the water. Then the fish rush forward to catch the fruit as it sinks, crunching it up in their powerful jaws. Fish such as piranhas and the tambaquí are important dispersers of the seeds of many rain forest trees.

◄ Chimpanzees love to feed on fruit. This helps disperse the seeds of the fruit trees.

13

Buried treasure

Clark's nutcracker feeds mainly on the seeds of the piñon pine. It teases the seeds from the cones of the pine. Then it splits them open. During the fall, a single bird gathers between 20,000 and 30,000 seeds to eat in the depths of winter. It flies all around, burying the seeds in the ground four or five at a time. The nutcracker memorizes tiny details of the landscape to help it find its secret stores later. But the bird cannot remember every hiding place. In the spring, some of the uneaten stashes begin to sprout, and a few grow into new piñon pines. In return for its winter feast, the nutcracker helps spread the tree's seeds through the forest.

◄ *A Clark's nutcracker perches on a piñon pine tree.*

Hitching a ride

Animals ignore the seeds of some plants because they taste bad. These seeds sometimes disperse by hitching a ride instead. When broad-leaved plantain seeds get wet, they become coated in a sticky liquid. The liquid helps the seeds attach to passing animals. Most plant hitchers, however, do not use glue to hang on. Cocklebur seeds, for example, have tiny hooks that cling tightly to animal fur or feathers or to people's clothing.

Devil's claw plants grow among the sand dunes of the Kalahari Desert in southern Africa. Their seed pods have sharp hooks that stick to the hooves of antelopes. As the antelopes wander away, they crush the Devil's claw seed pods. This helps scatter the seeds.

◄ *An antelope may unwittingly help a Devil's claw plant disperse its seeds.*

▼ *The grappling hooks of a Devil's claw plant attach seed pods to passing animals.*

Double trouble

It makes no difference to a Devil's claw plant which kind of antelope scatters its seed pods—any will do. Other types of plants must use a particular animal to scatter their fruit or seeds. Partnerships between a single plant and a single animal are risky. If one partner becomes **extinct** (dies out), the other is in serious trouble.

The tambalacoque tree used to flourish on the island of Mauritius in the Indian Ocean. Its fruits were eaten by large, flightless birds called dodos. Stones in the dodo's gut ground away at the surface of the tough tambalacoque seeds. The grinding enabled the seeds to sprout when they passed out of the bird to the forest floor. When the last dodo died in about 1681, the seeds had no way of sprouting. So no new tambalacoque trees grew. By the 1970s, only 13 trees were still alive. Then scientists had the idea of feeding some seeds to domestic turkeys. The seeds sprouted, and the endangered tambalacoque tree was saved.

▲ *Seeds of a tambalacoque tree needed to pass through the gut of a dodo before they could sprout.*

15

KEY FACTS

■ Without animal pollinators, we would have no apples, cherries, carrots, or chocolate.

■ A honeybee may gather more than two million pollen grains on a single feeding trip.

■ During the day, hummingbirds must drink nectar every 15 minutes to keep flying.

■ A Clark's nutcracker can remember where it buried its seed hoards for up to nine months.

Sharing **SPACE** and **BODIES**

All animals need somewhere safe to raise their young. Many share the homes of other animals to breed. A few even grow up inside a different creature's body. There are insects that grow inside starfish, birds that nest with termites, and fish that need mussels to breed.

Many animals need the help of other animals to breed. Sometimes different animals share nests. Some animals invade the bodies of others to lay their eggs inside, while the young of many insects grow inside dung deposited by larger animals.

Ball games

Many dung beetles make edible nests out of dung dumped by grazing mammals. The beetles use their strong front legs to gather dung into lumps the size of golf balls. They roll the balls away and bury them underground for their young to feed on. A dung beetle can bury 250 times its own weight in dung in just one night.

Farmers benefit from having dung beetles on their land. Some flies that bite cattle breed in cow dung. Fewer flies live in areas where the cows'

◀ *A dung beetle rolls a ball of elephant dung away from rival beetles. The ball will provide food and a home for the beetle's young.*

No mussel, no fish

Bitterling fish can only breed with the help of swan mussels, which are a type of freshwater shellfish. The male and female bitterling mate close to one of the mussels. The mussel vacuums up their fertilized eggs through its breathing tube. After two or three weeks of development the eggs hatch, and the mussel releases the baby fish.

But the mussel has a trick up its sleeve. While the bitterlings are mating, it pumps out lots of its own young. Some of the young mussels hook on to the female bitterling's skin. For three months they suck juices from her body. Then, the miniature mussels drop off and sink to the bottom.

▲ *A pair of bitterling court beside a swan mussel. The fish and the mussel will exchange young.*

18

▼ *This two-toed sloth only visits the ground to defecate.*

dung is harvested by beetles. Dung beetles also help turn over the soil and make it fertile, helping plants grow. Grazing mammals are unaffected by this relationship, but the beetles benefit. Biologists call this a **commensal** relationship.

Life in the slow lane

Sloths are slow-moving mammals that browse on leaves in rain forest trees. Many tiny animals live on their bodies, including some very strange moths. The adult moths live on the sloth, but their caterpillars live and feed in sloth dung. Sloths come down from the trees about once a week to defecate at the base of a tree. The moths grab this opportunity. They jump from the sloth to lay eggs on the fresh dung. When the young moths become adults, they fly away to find a sloth home of their own.

Mobile homes

Some animals use the bodies of larger animals as safe homes for their young. The young of many freshwater mussels, for example, develop on the bodies of fish. This helps stop them from drifting downstream. The young of the shiny-ray pocketbook mussel develop in a fish-shaped pouch at the end of a long, transparent thread. The adult mussel waves the thread in the current. This lures a hungry largemouth bass, which gulps down the pouch. The young mussels break free to develop on the **gills** of the bass.

Marine caddisflies are another group of creatures that use other animals as nurseries. These insects breed in rock pools around the coasts of Australia. A female caddisfly injects her eggs through tiny holes on a starfish's arms. The caddisfly

▲ *A female handfish guards her clutch of eggs, which is attached to a sea squirt.*

▼ *A shiny-ray pocketbook mussel tempts a bass to swallow its young.*

larvae soon hatch. They live inside the starfish for a while before leaving through the holes in the arms. The larvae complete their development in the rock pool. They live inside cases made of sand to thwart **predators.**

A sticky situation

For some animals, finding somewhere safe to lay eggs is a tough job. The spotted handfish lives in shallow, sandy bays where there are few rocks or coral to attach its eggs to. The fish has a neat solution to this problem. It lays its eggs on a sea squirt. Sea squirts are jelly-like animals that live fixed to the seabed. The female handfish uses her stiff fins to amble across the seafloor. When she finds a suitable sea squirt, she glues a sticky mass of eggs on top. The handfish guards the sea squirt for two months until the baby fish hatch.

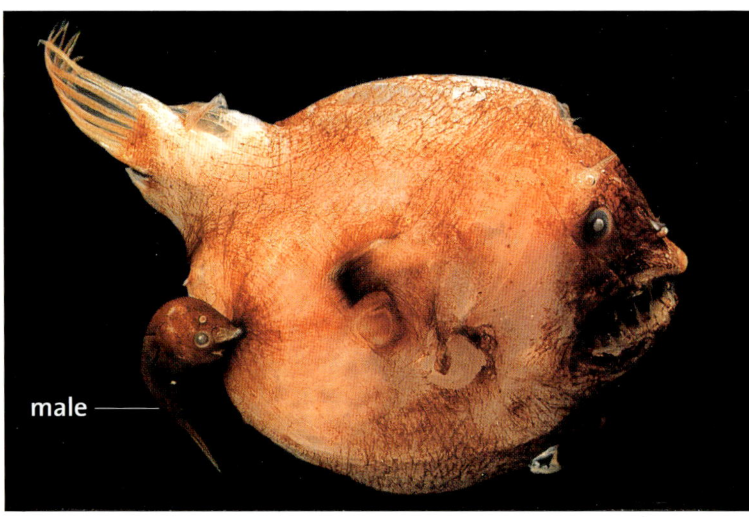

▲ *This female anglerfish has a tiny male attached to her body.*

Ultimate partners

For deep-sea anglerfish, the main problem is not where to breed but how to find a mate. These fearsome fish lurk up to 13,000 feet (3,960 m) below the surface of the sea. Locating a mate in the dark ocean depths is not easy. So when a male anglerfish bumps into a female, he grips her with his sharp teeth and holds on tight. The male is dwarfed by his partner. He is about 4 inches (10 cm) long, while she may reach more than 3 feet (0.9 m) in length.

The male absorbs food from the female's blood and begins to merge with her body. Gradually he loses his eyes, jaws, fins, and tail. The male becomes a permanent part of the female, living as a **parasite** on her body.

Trading places

Making a nest can be hard work, so many animals take over one that is ready-made. Woodpeckers drill nest holes in tree trunks.

▶ *A buff-breasted paradise kingfisher perches beside the entrance to its nest, which lies inside a termite mound.*

As soon as the woodpeckers move out, other animals move in. Owls, bats, squirrels, opossums, and ducks all breed in old woodpecker holes. Small birds such as chickadees also nest in empty holes left by woodpeckers. They make the entrance narrower by plastering mud around it until it is just the right size.

Castles of clay

Chickadees nest in lots of places, including odd locations such as mailboxes. But some birds are far more fussy—they only use the home of a particular animal. The golden-shouldered parrot of Australia nests only in termite mounds. During the day, it nibbles a hole in the side of a mound to create an egg chamber.

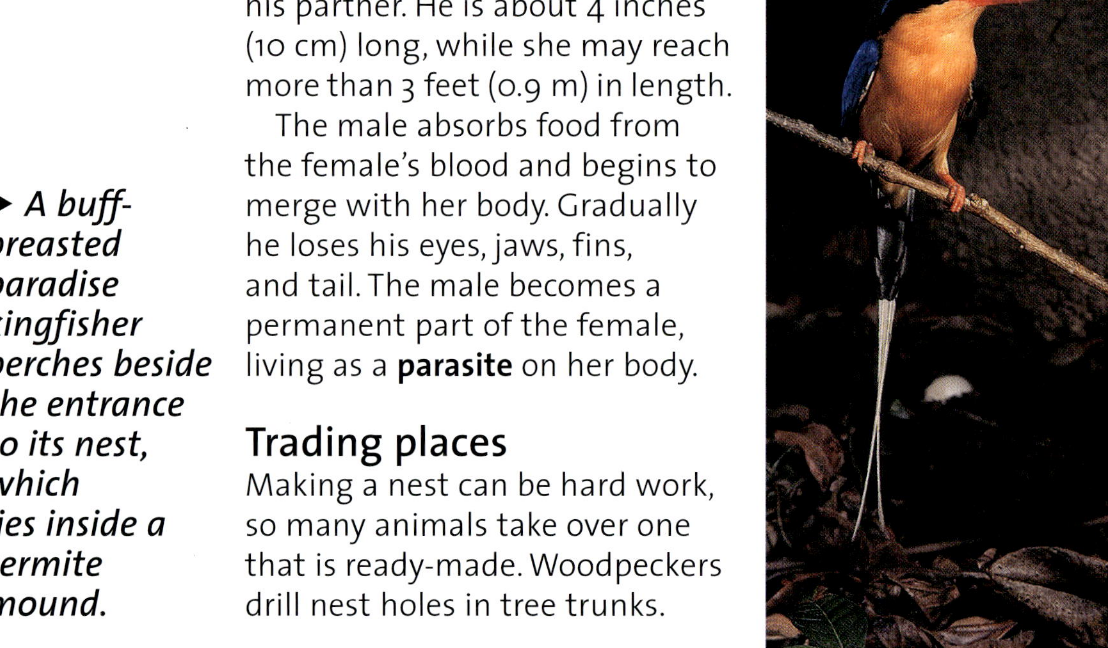

At night, armies of angry termites repair the damage with tiny pieces of clay. If the parrot tries enough times, the termites eventually allow it to use part of their mound. But sometimes the termites brick in the parrot chicks, which soon starve.

Many other animals use termite mounds for a nest. The world's largest bee, Wallace's lost bee, lives on just a few islands in Southeast Asia. Teams of adult female bees work together, using their giant mouthparts to dig a nest in the walls of a termite mound. Inside the nest, each female builds a series of cells using chips of wood mixed with tree sap. The female bees lay eggs inside their cells, and provide a store of **pollen** for their young.

Odd couples

Lack of space may force different animals to raise their families together. The sooty shearwater is a bird that flies over the ocean for most of the year. After nine months at sea, it returns to islands off the coast of New Zealand to breed.

But while the shearwater is away, its burrow may be occupied by a reptile called a tuatara. The bird cannot dig a new hole because every inch of space is already taken by other burrows. So it shares its nest instead. The bird lays its egg at the base of the tunnel, while the tuatara stays near the entrance.

▲ *Female Wallace's lost bees dig a nest in a termite mound. These giant bees are as long as an adult person's thumb!*

21

KEY FACTS

■ Small birds often build their nests on the edges of eagle and stork nests.

■ In Africa, dwarf mongooses often make nests inside termite mounds.

■ Some dung beetles feed their grubs a mixture of manure, fruit, and decaying meat.

■ In one species of deep-sea anglerfish, the female is up to 500,000 times larger than the male.

Cheats and
TRICKSTERS

Cheating is a way of life for many animals. They fool other animals into looking after their young, allowing the cheats to concentrate on laying more eggs. Some plants also use a trick or two to help them deceive the animals that pollinate them.

Rather than go to the trouble of building a nest and raising young, some birds let others do all the work. They lay eggs in the nests of their **hosts** and leave them to raise their chicks. Birds like these are called **brood parasites.** Brood parasitism is a rare way for birds to breed. There are almost 9,700 species of birds in the world, but only about 100 of them are brood parasites.

Risky business

Birds that are brood parasites trick other birds into accepting their eggs and caring for their young. This is a risky strategy. **Foster parents** often remove or eat brood parasite eggs. They may also abandon the nest if they think something is wrong. If this happens, all the eggs get cold and fail to hatch.

Using foster parents is a gamble, but there are many advantages. Unlike

▲ A young cuckoo catfish peers out from inside the mouth of its cichlid host.

Rough and tumble

A baby Eurasian cuckoo kills its rivals before they even hatch. A newly hatched cuckoo is naked, blind, and helpless. Although it is weak, it has a powerful urge to hurl everything else out of the nest.

The cuckoo nestling rocks from side to side to push an egg off the floor of the nest. Then it heaves the egg over the side. This requires an immense effort. But the nestling keeps going until all the eggs of the host birds are gone.

Having pushed out the hosts' eggs, the cuckoo chick is alone in the nest. Now it can gulp down all the food its foster parents bring back.

▶ *Although the gray cuckoo egg stands out against the blue host eggs, the host is fooled nonetheless.*

24

▼ *A female great spotted cuckoo. She will wait for her victims to leave their nest before swooping in.*

other birds, brood parasites do not have to build a nest, **incubate** (keep warm) their eggs, or feed their young. They can devote all their energy to producing eggs and visiting many nests instead. Female brood parasites produce more eggs than other birds.

Cowbirds, for example, can lay up to 80 eggs in a single season. Only a domestic chicken, bred for egg laying, can beat this record.

Hatching a plan

Brood parasites are expert tricksters. The female great spotted cuckoo hides until her victims leave their nest. She swoops down and lays an egg in the nest, before dashing away. The whole operation takes less than ten seconds—too fast for the hosts to notice.

Other cuckoos create a diversion. A male pied cuckoo flaps slowly past the nest of a pair of bulbuls. The angry bulbuls take off to chase away the much larger intruder.

▲ This yellow warbler has fed a juicy caterpillar to a cowbird chick, which is much larger than the warbler's real young.

Female Eurasian cuckoos use warblers, wrens, and other insect eaters. This is because their nestlings need a lot of tasty caterpillars and bugs. Brown-headed cowbirds, which live throughout the United States, are less fussy. They lay their eggs in the nests of 220 different species, including warblers, flycatchers, finches, robins, and cardinals.

Meanwhile, the female pied cuckoo slips quietly into the unoccupied nest. She removes one of the bulbuls' eggs and replaces it with one of her own.

Spot the difference

Bulbuls happily look after the large white eggs of pied cuckoos, even though their own eggs are small and brown. Like most birds, bulbuls simply count how many eggs are in the nest. As long as the right number is there, they continue to incubate as normal.

Brood parasites must choose foster parents that feed their chicks the right kind of food.

Chick or cheat

The chicks of brood parasites use a range of tactics to get more food than their nest mates. They are usually noisier and larger. They also have huge gaping mouths, which are bright red or orange inside. The foster parents cannot resist the loud chirping and colorful mouths of the imposters and give them more than their fair share of food.

Scrambled eggs

Some brood parasites target other birds of their own species. Wood ducks

▶ Adult cowbirds need a lot of insects. They live around herds of animals such as buffalo. Many tasty insects grow inside buffalo dung.

25

nest in holes in trees. There is often a shortage of suitable holes. So a female wood duck may sneak into another female's nest and lays her eggs there. This allows the duck to avoid having to rear her young, so she can go on to lay more eggs instead. However, this can backfire. Sometimes a parasitized female deserts her nest. Then none of the eggs inside will hatch.

Unwelcome guests

Not all brood parasites are birds. Mojave desert weaver spiders lay their eggs on their webs before they die in the fall. Tiny jumping spiders then sneak in and lay eggs of their own. In spring, the jumping spiders' eggs hatch first. The young jumping spiders feast on the weaver spiderlings.

There are also many insect brood parasites. Cuckoo bees invade other bees' nests and lay their eggs there. They mainly attack solitary bees, but some invade the hives of honeybees and bumblebees. Workers inside the hive tend both the cuckoo bee eggs and the eggs of their own queen. Some cuckoo bees sneak quietly into their victims' nest. Others fight their way in and kill any worker bees that try to stop them. When the cuckoo bee **larvae** hatch, they massacre the other young bees and take control of the entire nest.

26

◄ *The bird that this young wood duck will follow from its nest may not be its true mother. Female wood ducks often lay eggs in other wood duck's nests.*

Masters of deception

You probably know that adult stick insects are expert mimics. They look just like leaves or twigs to fool **predators**. But it is not just the adults that use deception to trick other animals.

Female stick insects flick away their eggs, which drop down to the ground. The eggs mimic seeds and have a tiny button attached to the top. This contains nutrients that ants adore. The ants carry the eggs to their nests. They break off the tasty button but toss the rest of the egg aside. The eggs develop in the safety of the ants' nest for a few months. When the young stick insects hatch, they look and behave just like ants. The real ants ignore them, allowing the stick insects to crawl outside. Then they climb into nearby trees and shrubs and start feeding.

◀ *As ants bring seedlike stick insect eggs into their nest, an antlike young stick insect scurries out.*

Some insects are brood parasites of their own species. Eggplant lace bugs lay round clusters of eggs and guard them until they hatch. Some sneaky females add their own eggs to other females' clusters. The sneaks' eggs are cared for. This leaves the rogue females free to lay more eggs.

A fishy tale

One type of fish, the cuckoo catfish from Lake Tanganyika in East Africa, uses other fish to care for its young. The catfish is a brood parasite of cichlid fish. Female cichlids carry their eggs inside their mouths. There, the eggs are kept safe from predators and are supplied with **oxygen.**

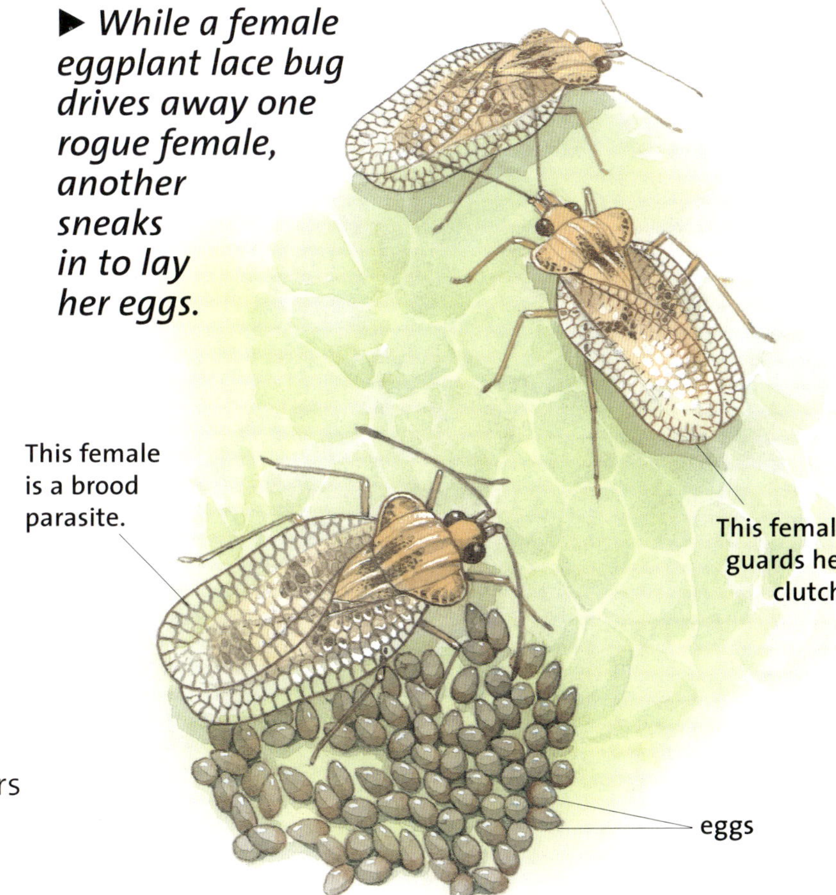

▶ *While a female eggplant lace bug drives away one rogue female, another sneaks in to lay her eggs.*

This female is a brood parasite.

This female guards her clutch.

eggs

The cichlid is tricked into looking after the eggs of the catfish as well as its own. The catfish releases its eggs at the same time as the cichlid. The cichlid draws its eggs into its mouth and takes in those of the catfish, too.

The young catfish hatch from their eggs in just three days, several days before the cichlids. The catfish feast on the cichlid eggs. When the remaining cichlid eggs begin to hatch, the young catfish eat the baby cichlids, too.

Daylight robbery

Animals don't just trick each other. Some cheat flowering plants by stealing **nectar** without bothering to carry the plants' **pollen**. Carpenter bees, for example, slice into the bases of flowers with their mouthparts. They take the nectar without getting dusted with pollen. These bees are not **pollinators**—they are thieves.

Flower piercers have also turned to a life of crime. These brightly colored birds use their hooked bills to slash flowers open. Their beak work soon reduces the blooms to shreds. The flower piercers then feed on the flower nectar.

▲ A cuckoo catfish blends in with gravel on the lake bottom.

▼ A flower piercer sizes up a meal of tasty flower nectar.

28

Phony flowers

Some plants fool animals into helping them **reproduce.** These plants tempt the animals to **pollinate** them but offer nothing in return. A few flowers are fakes with no nectar. They trick animals into visiting because they look like other flowers that do offer a nectar reward.

Many plants exploit bees to ensure pollination. Some orchids are shaped like enemy insects, and hostile bees try to attack them. During the struggle, the orchids smear pollen over the bees. The bucket orchid takes bees prisoner. It uses a kind of trapdoor to dump the bees into a tiny chamber. There is only one exit, which forms a narrow tunnel. As the bees squeeze themselves through the tunnel, the orchid glues its pollen onto their backs.

Deceiving bees

Perhaps the sneakiest deceiver of bees is the mirror orchid. This plant has a strong perfume that smells just like a female bee. The flower also bears a bright blue patch that looks like a female bee's shiny wings. Male bees are fooled by the plant. Thinking it is a female bee, they land on the flower and try to mate with it. Pollen brushes on to the bee during the scuffle. The confused bees then take the pollen to the next mirror orchid they fall for.

KEY FACTS

■ One percent of the world's birds are brood parasites, which lay their eggs in the nests of other birds.

■ Some types of African cuckoos can lay more than 20 eggs in quick succession.

■ Greater honeyguides are brood parasites. Their chicks kill other nestlings with a hook on their bill.

■ Cuckoo ants build their own tiny nest inside the much larger nests of other types of ants.

▼ *The flowers of this mirror orchid look and smell like a female bee.*

29

Things to Do

Testing bee vision

How do bees know which flowers to visit? Here is an easy experiment you can do in your backyard to find out. Make sure you get an adult to help you.

You will need two sheets of plastic or plastic-coated paper. One should be red and the other blue. Snip one of the sheets into a flower shape. Use this shape as a template to cut out the other. These will become fake flowers with which

◀ *This worker bee is collecting nectar and pollen for its nest mates. You can fool bees with plastic flowers and a dab of honey.*

you will trick the bees. Next, put a drop of honey into the center of each of the plastic flower shapes. Place them on the ground near a flowerbed. In time, bees will begin to land to take some of the honey. Watch closely and see which of the phony flowers attracts the bees. Be careful not to get too close to the bee as it collects the honey—if the insect feels threatened it might try to sting you.

When you have decided which colors bees see best, take a look at real flowers in your backyard. Which ones do you think will be pollinated by bees? Can you think of any animals in your neighborhood that might pollinate the others?

Books and websites

■ Green, Jen. *Small Worlds: In a Backyard.* New York: Crabtree, 2002.

■ Holmes, Anita. *How Flowers Bloom.* Tarrytown, NY: Benchmark Books, 2000.

■ *See through a bee's eyes at:* http://cvs.anu.edu.au/andy/beye/beyehome.html

■ *Learn about the wonderful world of insects at:* http://www.earthlife.net/insects/six.html

Words to Know

brood parasite
Animal that tricks another into caring for its young

commensalism
Relationship between two creatures in which one benefits but the other is unaffected

dispersal
Movement of organisms to new areas

extinct
When an entire species (type of organism) dies out

fertilize
When male sex cells fuse with female sex cells called eggs

foster parent
Animal that cares for the young of another

gills
Feathery organs used by many underwater animals to draw oxygen gas from the water

host
Animal or plant that supports a parasite or a commensal organism

incubate
To keep the eggs of a bird warm

larva
Young of an insect such as a fly (plural: larvae)

mutualism
Relationship between two creatures in which both partners benefit

nectar
A sugary liquid produced by plants to reward pollinators

organism
Any type of living thing, including plants, animals, bacteria, and fungi

oxygen
Gas that all animals and plants need to live

parasite
Any organism that benefits at the expense of another

pollen
Plant powder that contains male sex cells

pollination
Transfer of pollen from one plant to another

pollinator
Animal that takes pollen from flower to flower

predator
Animal that hunts and eats other animals

proboscis
Strawlike tube through which butterflies and moths suck up liquids

reproduction
The act of producing offspring

symbiosis
Close relationship between different types of creatures (plural: symbioses)

ultraviolet light
Light that is invisible to people but can be seen by animals such as insects

Index

Numbers in *italics* refer to pictures